EMERGENCIES OF THE
Heart

Poems

LESLIE MCGRAW

EMERGENCIES OF THE HEART

Copyright © 2014 by Leslie McGraw

All rights reserved. No part of this publication may be reproduced, stored in a retrieval system, or transmitted in any form, or by any means, electronic, mechanical, recording, photocopying or otherwise without the prior written permission of the publisher.

Anthem Program

Aquarius Press

PO Box 23096

Detroit, MI 48223

www.aquariuspress.net/anthem

ISBN 978-0-9897357-7-3

Printed in the United States of America

In memory of the victims that lost their lives on September 11, 2011.

Dedicated to the survivors who will never be the same and for my son, Marc—my reason for survival.

Dear Bill,

Thank you so much for supporting me in life and poetry. I appreciate your service to America and your critique for poems.

Leslie McGraw

EMERGENCIES OF THE HEART

Introduction	7
No Chicken Soup	9
Corporate Eden	11
Missing Person (an interview)	12
Beams of Light	13
Time is Like a Dream	14
The Giver	15
Finding Peace in a Natural World	16
Sun n Snow	17
Like Rain	19
The Usual	20
The Firefly	22
Imagine	23
I Can't	27
Unleashed	28
I shouldn't be here	31
Homeless	32
Bloated	34
Nothing Tastes As Good	35
Divided By Two	36
Kiss Me and Make It Better	37
Think Twice	39
Just a friend who makes me smile	42
A Promise with No Name	43
"Hey Momma . . ."	47
Kid Fear	49
Blank Pages and Empty Rooms	50
Getting Peace: An Open Letter	52
Learning	55
Four Thousand, Five Hundred, Twenty-eight Days	56
Releasing Your Inner Sheba	57
I Dare You	59
The Like Button	60
Still in Love: A Peace to Be Spoken	61

Thank You   62
Acknowledgments   64
About The Author   66

INTRODUCTION

"There's only one person we have to live with our entire lives and that is ourselves." –Dr. Sandra Wray-McAfee

Every generation of Americans has at least one moment where young adults are faced with the worst and best of humanity on a national scale. For me, it was the demolition of the twin towers.

Eventually, I came to understand that my acute reaction was, in part, because it gave me the permission to grieve my own disappointments and losses without being labeled, judged, or alienated.

This is not a book about 9-11 and death. This is a book about life, love, purpose, hope, and the valuation of time—all of which I have assessed differently since the events that occurred on 9-11. As the new towers have gone through the stages of the best and the brightest, to the lowest…to Ground Zero, and now back to an inspiring tower of freedom, I am encouraged to move forward in love and stand tall in power with new hopes and expectations.

9-11, and my own processing of the events and the aftermath, set my own personal journey, via the journaling that helped me to explore and evaluate my own heart. During the first years, most of my journaling had to deal with my emotions—how I felt about this or that. Once I started to mine those journals, I found something deeper, beyond the flesh. During this twelve-year process of mining journals for spoken word, spoken word for poetry to share on the page, I discovered beauty and dirt about myself.

Preparing these poems reminded me that I survived some of my worst times with my soul intact. Speaking with a poet friend, Katherine Edgren, was the final pearl that stringed these thoughts together. I told her I did not understand why people watched scary movies. She said it was because when you make it to the end of the scary movie, it means "I survived."

I.

Not in the clamor of the crowded street,
Not in the shouts and plaudits of the throng,
But in ourselves, are triumph and defeat

—Henry Wadsworth Longfellow

No Chicken Soup

The rubies earthed in
the hub of the rubble
leave behind a tiny fire
that helps me breathe

when there is no fresh air,
when all the industrial-strength
helpers have
gone home and the

honorary volunteers glide in
with thick noodles of comfort
and moist cobbler baked
with tears and berries.

I don't want no chicken soup

to soothe my soul. I want to
keep it roaring, awake and ready
to meet this new fusion of life and
death, these new terms of survival.

Keeping up with the city beat, but
lingering long enough to
sense her being in my center. I am
getting used to these fast-type blues

crying in rhyme,
on cue
at the unscheduled time
when the bop-bop-bop stops

at night I can almost feel her touch,
hear her accent lingering
between the notes, life and disaster.

And I don't want no chicken soup
drowning it out.

Corporate Eden

A few minutes before nine,
we looked straight past
the receptionist
to the temporary
broadcasting station
from the Big Apple.

We stood together
talking,
shouting,
then whispering,
before the silence
of three thousand

instant funerals
crashed down on us.
Panic crawled throughout
our flesh as the contrail
of death and news
bled through the TV.

Tough-stuff JoAnna,
our office New Yorker,
crumpled with the grief
uncertainty assigns
to family.

Deadlines and politics
shifted inside
networks of office cubicles
superficially protected by
an open door and
an information counter.

Now, everything is different.

Missing Person (an interview)

—Sharon Vanzie, a New York City native, lived in the same apartment complex as a high-school classmate, who was reported missing from the 104th floor of the World Trade Center.

"From a human standpoint, it was devastating. The day after, you saw flyers all over the place of people who were missing. We were inundated with this every day. Every, every day.

The next day I saw the flyer about my high school acquaintance. Her husband posted it; he had to keep hope that maybe she had gotten out. When I saw the flyer I just started to cry."

Beams of Light

I still smell death
when the breeze enters
the apartment, hear chaos
as I close my blinds.

As I close my eyes
I can see light through
my weepy, webbed
and bruised eyelids.

Two beams illuminate the sky
with hope for a new day.
Two little beams shine from the kid's
room, in hopes of a fairytale ending.

Time is Like a Dream

Everything was so clear, so vivid
so real.
You were there,
It was your reality.

Out of the moment
all you remember is the emotion,
the jumbo picture with
jagged, yellowed edges.

But the end is so clear. Bloody
hands balled into fists, terror
ripping through your body as you fall,
metal grinding between teeth.

After the end
you can't remember.
Now that the senses have relaxed,
you can't hear the arguments.

All that remain are pictures,
theories and heated last words.
It's either pain or smiles;
nothing in between.

Does time heal all wounds?
Or does it just blur the details
and give you more life to grieve,
to grasp "reality" a scene at a time?

The Giver

Death is necessary
for us to live. Life recycles–
as one loses life,
One gives.

Finding Peace in a Natural World

Aka: The Persecuted Church

Coded thoughts and ideas:
an etiquette for hope,
faith teetering on possession.

A man-made norm, a global
web of thought, logic, ethics, codes
cracked, hacked and killed

before maturity.

How you behave, the joy shared
in each hello, the way you disagree
is the God we all see before we know.

You are, I am, WE ARE the Church.
Don't blame the Internet or the news.
The persecution starts in the pews.

Sun n Snow

The floor is hard and cold,
finite.
The ceiling is bright and bold,
infinite...
sun and snow
defined.

An imperfect pair,
yet the perfect team.
Storms and confusion,
physical beauty
and vain dreams
lasting only a season.

A youthful spring heart,
prematurely grey,
dances through a short summer.
Too busy to reflect,
to eavesdrop
on park benches.

Fooled by the brilliant colors
of dead and lonely leaves,
she is readying for a day
while he settles
before the ground is covered
white. Shimmery reflections

with resolutions
to move forward...
If God gave second chances.
If God forgave easier than the human heart.

On a Valentine Day
the floor is soft and cold,
a blessing.

The ceiling is warm and bold,
a promise
that spring will return.

Like Rain

It clears away all the
scales and debris
so I can see when
the sun shines
again.

The sun listens,
shining quietly-
yet too distant to trust.

My emotions run like
syrup and vinegar
and my smile wears out
at points during the day,
but my joy is constant –
replenished day by day,
Like rain.

The Usual

I took a nap.
Then I woke up
feeling refreshed with a giggle
bursting my insides,
so social it had to be freed.

I picked up my phone
to key the usual digits
to the usual person.
But then I remembered
I won't be having any more
usual days.

So I lay back on my pillow
with a tense
wave of grief
and a sore chest
from this unusual place.

What do I do with this
boredom
shaped from
pain and grief?
Procrastinating…

I heal with each letter
that comes to me. Pushing
through the necessaries,
I sift through unfrosted bits
hoping for a morsel of the familiar.

If I had never been through it before,
I would think I was dying.
But, because I have
I will
just keep trying...

the only way I know how.
To write through it,
To press on until
I find something familiar
again.

The Firefly

At the tip –
Hope raised glittery
dust from the underground.

We warmed up to the idea
of late nights and bright lights.
Memories of his
nostalgia of her
back when
she was
free and on fire.

Delicately dancing
through life,
sensually syncopated
around the
threat
of being
s q u a s h e d.

Youthful and wise,
a jazz of survival
she taught him
before dreams were
assassinated
by the movement
of other's freedoms.

Now dead,
but not gone.
She just integrated …

Imagine

I want you all to join me
in a moment of silence…
I am the ears that hear
the emergencies – your 9-1-1
operator.

Now,
as you open your eyes,

IMAGINE
A woman working in the Pentagon
at the time the plane
erupted into a fire that would leave
her skeleton, still holding her pen.

IMAGINE
The lives censored that day
All the voices silenced,
hurtful memories of 9-11.

IMAGINE
The shameful loss of Katrina
Sybrina and Trayvon,
their history gone…

IMAGINE
Parents losing hope
on their own kids
using dope,
and no name
to erase all feeling.

IMAGINE
People re-elect the son of sin
and name the next Antichrist.
Nobody wins,

Nobody listens.

Now IMAGINE
If you couldn't speak…

If you didn't have <u>no</u> voice
In your country
'cuz you don't have a presence
In your city
'cuz nobody on your block voted
For a mayor who would give a
Fuck whether you got street
Lights or police
In yo' hood
'cuz more people showed up to march
than to vote
for a state rep to present
welfare and traffic laws.

Even if
you didn't need them
Even if
you didn't have the network
Even if
you didn't have money
to donate.

If you didn't have a voice
AT WORK
'cuz you didn't learn how to
Speak bi-negro
Or buy the right shirt
AT SCHOOL
You didn't have a voice in the
PTO and the mommas
making the decisions didn't
have kids that looked like yours.

IMAGINE
You could speak again
What would you say?
Would you talk about, who's gay?
Or how much you weigh?
What would you have to say?

Think of me
as your 9-1-1 operator.
What do you have to say?
You don't know how long
you have to speak.

It's an EMERGENCY
Are you okay?
Are you okay?
Are you able to speak?
What do you have to say?

II.

"The poet is a reporter interviewing his own heart."

—Christopher Morley

I Can't

This ugly in-between,
this horrid cast of extras.
Everything that we
built up has fallen,
and looking back

I can't feel

bad as I did that day.
Nor can I hope as grand
as the first day
I began.
I discovered=
when I laid
my eyes on you.

Unleashed

i.

Why do we keep dogs on a leash?
What would happen if we let them free?
Would they snap and attack?
Or run and play and then come home

Why do we keep our hearts on a leash
releasing love only as far as the eyes can see?
What if we set it free?
Would it run wild?

Why do we make such an effort to protect, to restrain
ourselves from everything?
The heart is an animal –
raw and untamed
Like a dog.

ii.

Days of perfection
temper
years of rejection

leading to conception,
deception and lies
covered in bridal lace

masking your face.
Embraced in
legitimacy, finally

I was in a sacred place.
(I thought).
Your soul mate

                              (you thought)
                    before ejection you had
                    all love could contain.

iii.

I prayed for you
I prayed for us
I prayed for the babies

trying not to hurt
falling out exhausted
'fore I could pray for me.

But you couldn't resist,
change
your fate. Marking her territory

for a moment
you gave up freedom,
your overseer named.

Still mad cuz I ain't…
tamed. I am becoming
the bitch we both hate.

As you lick off the stains,
tongue-and-groove
I twist
with each reflection - afraid
I might find emptiness
inside of a love confined,
overflowing
with resentment
I remain.

iv.

Why do you keep a dog on a leash?
What would happen if you let him free?
Would he snap and attack?
or would he run and play?
Would he come back?

Would you love
again?
Would you forgive
again?
I know -
Maybe I always knew
you'd come back home,
your heart would return.
Maybe I always knew
You are not the wild dingo
you thought you were.
You want to pet me again…
Like a dog.

But while you were out
my heart was left unleashed.
Survival rewrote our story.

I've
become unleashed.
Unglued,
unresponsive
to You.

I shouldn't be here

Why am I laying
on this side of the bed?
Why am I tucked in
between sheets of flowers and
patterns with hot pink trim?

I should be straddling
between the "he" and "she"
side of the bed gripping
gray and green
flannel sheets and
flattened pillows.

I shouldn't be falling asleep
in peace and quiet.
Bump beauty rest;
I need
exercise.

Homeless

I have always dreamed
about being with a man who's romantic.

He would sing to me and lay it on real thick
like oil slathered on canvass.

With no limits on spending
time to find One Hundred Ways.

Staring into my eyes, he'd touch me soft
and kiss me like ice cream like no one's around.

I've surfed The Net, looking for that
certain somewhere romantic.

Dreaming
about romance and making love

exploring
as I put him on like a glove.

He'd bring flowers, then shower,
washing away the golden scent.

In search of romance, I've received gifts,
squealing with friends "that was so romantic!"

Googling for romance, I just find more questions.
Is it all sentimental? Uncommitted flattery?

Maybe the missing part is that one
needs to be open enough to receive love.

Then once you add care to the equation
romance is just the reciprocal of love.

You remain the center of my romantic thoughts -
improved by your love, not changed by you.

Romance is a place I want to live and gray with you.
Only problem is I haven't yet found you.

Bloated

Sitting under the full clouds
I frown,
so full it hurts.
No matter whether it was sweet
going down
or forcefully swallowed.
Now
I am full of it.

And when it comes out,
all fists and feets,
ugly and exhausting,
I am worried about that day.
But worried for myself, now.
What if that day doesn't come quick enough?
What if all that love
turns
    S
   O
  U
R
eating away at my soul?
What if I stop caring
by the time I hear his ringtone?

What if I settle
with nothing
but a tight smile
through the pain and pressure
tightening around my chest.
I can't
breathe
I need
O
  U
    T.

Nothing Tastes As Good

Looking like Superman Ice Cream.
Screaming like a
loud t- shirt
freshly laundered with Febreze.

Smelling like a promise
kept by the chocolate son,
nothing looks as good as you taste
and nothing tastes as good as you feel.

Divided By Two

I wish I didn't dream.

Thick honey brown drifted cedar
used to carry us,
so simply,
the weight just got to be a little
too much.

I wish I didn't still
think about us

still.
I daydream about us often.

It may have been that it was
left open with no plan. Or me
trying to correct
all of our defects
and holes,

but I miss us.

I wish
we
could just be.
I got so much for us.

Am I a dreamer?
Maybe so.

Do I dream of you?
So close, so real.

Damn, I wish I didn't dream.

Kiss Me and Make It Better

The tree branches thresh against the window sill
swaying my insides.

I find no comfort
in the sun
smiling at my pain,
or the shadows it casts to
dance
at the failed debut of my
dreams.

The birds gossip about me in their native lingo.
They look down at me.
When the door opens
I greet my offender,
my eyes still petition for acceptance.

Kiss me and make it better.
I don't want to hurt this bad.
I am trying to forgive.

You dined recklessly
while I put myself on rations.
You left your dung and debris
on my young heart.

Now tamed and wounded,
I need you to kiss it, make it right.
Be careful;
the cuts are too fresh for sage.

As you kiss off the stains
and suckle the temporal flesh on my lips,
my heart squeaks as it pumps tears,
flushing away debris.

I flinch with each kiss,
delicately placing our love into
a familiar box
filled with resentment.
Kiss me. Make it better—
not just okay.

Think Twice

Take a minute
And think back to
That new
"Friend"
 In your life

NEXT.
You started thinking,
Or maybe you shoulda started thinking.
Maybe you shoulda thought twice.

We started out slow
Trying to get to know
Our new friend.

Every day
Every call
Every talk
Didn't have a start,
Didn't have an end.

Suddenly
More than friends
We started questioning.
Whining,
Demanding,
Wanna know
Where you at?
Where you been?
Who is that?
Wanna know
Who is she
Who was he
Is that yo' friend?
Whose is it?
What's my name?

What you cook?
Who's calling
On yo cell?
Wanna go
In the street
Come home beat
Back to me.
Wanna go
Out to eat
Dutch treat.
Where your keys?
You got some gas?
I want some azz.
NOW.

Later on
Wanna talk
On you cell
After dark
After 9.
After the game
Has been played.
What's up?

Now you rushing me?
Always in a hurry.

STRESSING ME!
Saying "Baby, don't worry."

Man…Let's take a minute.

Think Twice.
You seem nice.

But wassup?
Am I applying for marriage
Or is this an application for an interview

For a layaway plan?
If so, then how do you spell F.U. Man?

I wish I could write you a letter
To release all this...

So we can move forward
Like flowers,
Like partners,
Like lovers,
Facing in the direction of the sun
For protection.

In this thing,
there are no guarantees.
Is this really what you want?
Am I really what you need?

Just a friend who makes me smile

Just a friend who makes me smile
No Lines
No Dividers
No Patterns
No Pressure

Just a friend who makes me smile
A Thought
A Word
A Call
A Walk

A friend who makes me smile
One Touch
One Word
One Night
One Day

One friend who makes me smile
My Choice
My Teach
My Scholar
My Sweet

A Promise with No Name

(Dedicated to my Uncle Donnie Taylor for faithful service in Vietnam and our family)

This Goes Out to All the Unnamed Soldiers.
Groomed to survive
Like mammals
Fighting to stay alive
While taking lives
from anybody
Who was a threat
To His Life;
To His Promise for a better life,
For another's future.

Then Come Back to the American Way,
to starve in the land of prosperity,
to thirst,
until it became so unquenchable.
Alcohol blended with tears was the only solution
to drown away the blood path.
Up on the Ave,

Prescription Plan Two:
Get High
To even out
the Lows
Steering towards a path of busted dreams.

Walking down to the party store
Unarmed in his fatigues
Fighting wars
Within
Talking to his best friend
within himself.
Locked out by America,
Looked down on by America's Mothers,

Misunderstood by The People
Passing him by on the street safely
Because of the security
paid for by others just like him.

In Korea and Iraq
The Gulf and 'Vietnam way back
When did we forget?

This goes out to all the unnamed soldiers
Who think we have forgotten you
Like a receipt from a swap meet
in the 'hood and in the world.

I know it's killing you inside
But don't die.
Even though
I know we killing you
daily
with forgetfulness.

Please Don't Die
On your knees
At Church
Lift your head up to Jesus' shoulder
But don't die.

Even though
It's destroying you
at the reunion
when nobody says they are proud of you.
Please don't die!!
Even though
we kill you by not loving you
Please Don't Die.

Don't be another man down,
Don't fall to the unknown

ream of unnamed soldiers.
Because I love you and won't ever
forget.

III.

"... September 11 was a reminder that life is fleeting, impermanent, and uncertain. Therefore, we must make use of every moment and nurture it with affection, tenderness, beauty, creativity, and laughter."

—Deepak Chopra, M.D.

"**Hey Momma. I just called to give you that info you asked for real quick.**"

i.

"Hey Baby," she said slowly, dragging, changing the pace. "I saw you called earlier…" "Oh yeah. The reason I called was to give an update on the boy in the news that was killed." "Oh, okay. Did your friend, Sandra, make it over for her birthday

cake?" She spoke so slowly that my senses began to open up to the after-dinner aromas of black-eyed peas and lemon bar cake s-e-e-p-i-n-g into my soul. I let her finish her sentence out of courtesy; I already knew what she would ask. I always

knew. Her slow words gave me time to think of a quick answer so I didn't end up in a l-o-n-g conversation. "No; she didn't get back in time," I replied. She calmly breathed
                                        into the phone,

"Norma died."

ii.

The silence embraced us,
lingering after the
What
    (heart)
When
    (ten)
how
    (quickly)
she lost
    her best friend.

"I'm sorry baby,
    I know
        you have to

                    go—
                        I have a pencil to
                                take down that inf

At that moment
        I wished
                my reason to call
                                    had simply been to say
                    "I love you."

Kid Fear

There's a kid that lies in me
always scheming
big Star, big dreams
If I let her out,
the "Bigs" will get mad.
So, I shrink to a little within.

Mother Shirley used one of her last breaths
to warn me: "You're a dreamer; I can tell.
That's why they killed my son."
It's the first time she spoke to me regular.
I can't forget her last words,
her face was all wrinkled pain.

The dreamers are always under attack.
If they don't assassinate your dreams,
they'll just come and kill you instead.
Every tribe, farm, office and factory has
at least one –
the upstart with new ways, ideas.

I don't know if I want to protect my kid
or tell her just dream bigger.

Blank Pages and Empty Rooms

Moping 'til he came over
and bored me to sleep
and screwed me awake for a minute
or two.

An Empty Room

Before order.
Before responsibilities,
before dress codes,
sound, vibes, or style is checked -
before I have to wait.

Before rules.
before thoughts,
before form,
before words.
Before his story was written and produced.

A Blank Page

Before exposure
to style and elements.
Before aging
and time is released
with fury
like the Eve of Cain
and Abel is erased.

Before reality and statistics
cancelled possibilities
for the new and nameless,
dodging memories for
those on the margins.

Now that I've found the
power of blank pages,
I embrace my empty room
filled with space
to spread out and
collect the
originals.

Getting Peace: An Open Letter

Hey Cuz,

Wzp witcha? I hate to see you locked down for so long.
You've missed so much of what's been goin' on
In Iraq, in the schools…
And even wit yo' son.
Plus, wasting a good head like yours is wrong.
Everytime I talk to you, you lookin for something…
But you so busy trying to find SOMETHING
You losing what you had. You had peace within - -
Now you just trying to get a piece.
How we ever gone 'chieve
Real peace
When we rob, cheat and kill for
pieces?

Everybody wants a piece of
the action
But don't want to do
What it takes
To get it started
We settle for getting a piece of the action
AFTER
Plans and policies have been made.

Eating a portion of
Somebody else's leftovers
Every single day.

Don't you ever
Wonder
What would it feel like to taste the results?

From your own recipe?
From your own pot?
Not just a diluted sip

From the melting pot?
Why you settle?
Why you settling for pieces?

You said you was looking for a piece of mind.
Why you settle for a piece of mind
When you can do like T.D.
And get yo' self a He-motion
To help you grieve,
To move forward…
Why you settle?
Why you settling for pieces?
King had a dream about Rosa's nightmare..
And been rationed pieces of the Integrated American Dream
Ever since.
But waiting on A Dream Deferred
Is nonsense.

When you wake up
Your tomorrow
Is here today and
The American Way
Is to not get caught sleepin,
'Cuz while you sleeping
Others is taking
Making
And maintaining progress
While reaping, transporting
Migrating
Your Harvest.

Don't Fall, this is not yo' winter yet!
Get Yo' Piece
Of the pie because the dough was
Made from our hands
And our hard work.
FREE YOURSELF
I know

Your life ain't easy
And sometimes it hurts
But if you step Up
And take your foot off the nail it may work.

THIS TIME
I hope you hear me
THIS TIME
Scrappin' for scraps ain't gon' work.
FREE YOURSELF
Live
Life Like You are Loved
I'm waiting on you
I'm waiting for you
To get out of bondage.
Signed,
Yo' Cuz.

Learning

No matter who you are—
How old you are,
Who you aren't,
How young you aren't,
What your situation is,
What your situation ain't,

What choice you make,
How you deal
With and when
Things that happened,
Someone is learning from
You.

Four Thousand, Five Hundred, Twenty-eight Days

The blacker the bolder
           The blacker, the more emphasized
           The blacker, the more criticized

      It never gracefully hits the page. Never
can be used softly enough to erase or blend in
      To be presentable.
      Four Thousand, Five Hundred, Twenty-Eight Days
      New Black Ink Arrived
      My lil Black Ink
      Made History.

Four Thousand, Five Hundred Twenty-eight Days.
Not enough time to live
A whole lot of time to grow
For both of us.

Using black ink
To create new lines
New Form
New Ideas
New Ways

Four Thousand, Five Hundred, Twenty-Eight Days
Inerasable
Irreplaceable
Black Ink.

Releasing Your Inner Sheba

Aka Becoming a Vessel for Truth

I am Makeda.
Queen of Sheba
Born into distinction

A head above my peers.
Educated in Ethiopia
on a journey to find

My true love,
My true self.
My true worship

continues through a seed
a pomegranate,
sweet and full.

But none as sweet as the seed
ripened by the sun
which I adore. The sun,

who adores me,
who makes me, me.
Rich in strength,
power, and flavor,

even before I discovered the Circle
or Truth of Solomon—
the Truth inside me.
The quiet voice was

clearer than the roar. Once
I allowed myself to be
a vessel – guided,
I continue to explore

My true love.
My true self.
my majesty.

I Dare You

"For most of history, Anonymous was a woman."
—Virginia Woolf

You find inside
the woman
written by
the history of your next move—
a scheduled dream, a deep thought

liberated from time and forecasts,
the anonymous
to consider the unknown,
I dare you, my friend.

The Like Button

Obsessed with voting
up and down,
clinging to the visceral –
shameless selfies.

Daddies in uniform,
wretched mammas,
and babies in caskets
share the most.

This illustrious ideogram
confuses, compares,
comments and leads
voters to devour content.

Faithfully latching on to
the sites with the most Likes,
like Remora
waiting for motivation

or a discount
shared
at the expense of
the giver.

Still in Love: A Peace to Be Spoken

I am…
my heart.
I am my heart.
My heart ain't broken, just sore
so I wear protection. Now,
I'm untouched and neglected
limp and unfulfilled -

I grow
tired - but my heart don't.
I feel heartbroken,
but it ain't broke.
Brotha, I'm a weed.
Disappointment and stress
is what I feed

on and on.
It's what I needed
to get to this place
where you left me.
Still in love
with me.

I am
alone, turned wild -
illegitimate
once again. But
I survived
when the other flowers choked.

Thank You

Sitting on the pew as a child
with Mom and Grandma on each side,
smells of bacon and White Shoulders
penetrated the sanctuary

as latecomers were ushered
into wooden pews. I sat
like a soldier, stealing
mini naps, knowing full well

there were two hands and three sets of eyes
behind communion-white gloves and jeweled
bifocals waiting for me to act up so
we could visit that dreaded place "outside,"

ready for me to participate in hymns
with my mouth open wide reciting
the scripture and pep rally for tithes.
Most Sundays, services were pretty mild.

But on this particular day, the sermon about
Baby Moses had everyone wound up. Little
Ms. Samuels shuffled around the pews to the beat
of Melrose's organ prelude to "I Got a New Name."

Oh, but when the choir broke out into "over in Zion"
people put the hymnals down and stood
up shouting and doing the ugly cry

"Thankya Jesus!"
"Thankya Lawd!"

My grandma swayed and trembled with tears
and Aunt Carolyn yelled from the back pew.
Uncle Donnie pulled out a fresh hankie, stomping
the devil below the floorboards.

I scanned the crowd, trying to figure out
"Why was everyone so hyper?"
My shoulders tightened up, freezing me in my seat:
I didn't know if I should be scared or sad to see

the ones who taught me to keep composure
screaming through tears, waving their hands,
and pumping their fists. Today, I can't help but give
thanks for the memories, the tears, and the images.

Defeat didn't make them cry out;
Victory did.

ACKNOWLEDGMENTS

An earlier version of the poem, "Time for a Phone Call," was published in *Glimpses: A Peninsula Writers Anthology* in 2013. Earlier versions of "Sun n Snow," "Still in Love" and "Learning" have been published on my blog www.trustorysuccess.com. Earlier versions of "Finding Peace In A Natural World," "Releasing You Inner Sheba," "The Firefly," "Imagine," "Unleashed," "Kiss Me And Make It Better," "Think Twice," "A Promise With No Name," "Hey Momma," "Blank Pages and Empty Rooms," "Getting Peace," and "Four Thousand., Five Hundred, Twenty-Eight Days" have all been spoken before a live audiences across Southeast Michigan.

I would like to give thanks to the following people who allowed me to interview them about their personal stories surrounding the events on September 11, 2001: JoAnna DeCamp, Sharon Vanzie, and Dr. Bella G. Parker.

I would like to express my gratitude to the following people who have mentored, encouraged, and guided me through the process of finding the right method to articulate my message: Heather Buchanan-Gueringer, Crystos, Zilka Joseph, Natasha Trethewey, Jade Banks, Randall Horton, Dr. Deborah Mitchell, Nina Simmone, Karen Simpson, Charnita Thomas, Reanda Slay, Julia Bell, Laurita Thomas, Dr. Sandra Wray-McAfee, Carmen Wells-Quigg, Mary McCartney, and Mrs. Loomis (elementary librarians never had first names).

Next, I would like to thank everyone who has listened, given feedback and critique on my poetry. This includes the members, past and present, of the Ann Arbor Writers Group and the ATAMI (All Things Artistic Ministries, Inc.) Christian Writers Group. There are a few people I would like to mention by name as they have reviewed my poetry, listened to poems over the phone, at critique meetings, and at live events: Shelley Schanfield, Katherine Posselt, Dave Wanty, Skipper Hammond, Donnelly Wright Hadden, Kim Peters Fairley, Eleanor Andrews, Kate

Stone, Raymond Juracek, Stephanie Feldstein, Janet Cannon, Patricia Tompkins, Robyn Ford, Walter Ellerbe III, Joyce French, Kali Johnson, Sherlonya Turner, Megan Blackshear, Diane Wells, Tanya Solomon, Gayle, Don, David, and Christy.

Lastly, I would also like to thank the folks who have coached me through the personal growth and development that was necessary to search my heart for the right words. They have listened to me sort out emotions, poems over the phone, and at live events: Patricia McGraw (mom), Lester McGraw (Dad), George McGraw, Jr. (Uncle), Bertha L. Rowry (grandma), James McCartney, Rosanita Ratcliff, William Ratcliff, Bettye Ratcliff, Loretta Flowers, and Jacquie Bowman.

ABOUT THE AUTHOR

Leslie McGraw began sorting out her surroundings through writing in third grade following a move with her family to a new school district. She discovered her voice through the pen, maturing into a prolific performance poet, blogger, online content writer and freelance journalist. Today she lends this voice to advocacy, where she is passionate about helping others share their stories of struggle and victory as an empowering tool.

Leslie is a member of the Ann Arbor Writers Group, All Things Artistic Ministries, Inc. Writer's Group and The Peninsula Writers. She is also a recipient of The Leaven Center's Eleanor S. Morrison Scholarship for Creative Writing for Social Justice and the University of Michigan's Distinguished Diversity Leaders Award. She currently holds a Bachelor of Science in Business Management from the University of Phoenix, and an Associate of Business from Washtenaw Community College.

Leslie began sharing her poetry in the open mic arena and has been a featured spoken word poet across Southeast Michigan for over 14 years. Leslie has created content for dozens of companies including Buyer Zone, Bounty Paper Towels, and Lifescript and is the owner of the award-winning blog, Tru Story (www.trustorysuccess.com) and Life by Poetry (www.lifebypoetry.tumblr.com).